twitter

a pocket guide

Crombie Jardine
PUBLISHING LIMITED
Office 2
3 Edgar Buildings
George Street
Bath
BA1 2FJ
www.crombiejardine.com

First published by Crombie Jardine
Publishing Limited in 2009

ISBN 978-1-906051-37-2

Designed by Ben Ottridge
Printed in the UK by CPI William Clowes,
Beccles, NR34 7TL

contents

contents

"Just setting up my twttr"

*The first ever tweet, from Twitter
co-founder Jack Dorsey in 2006*

introduction

Twitter is a social networking site founded in 2006 and fast gaining popularity and momentum around the world. This pocket guide will help all those who want to join in the fun but haven't a clue where to start and will make sure novices are tweetwise in no time!

"I love how Twitter confirms my all too often assaulted belief that most humans are kind, curious, knowledgeable, tolerant and funny. Let's enjoy ourselves and to hell with those who don't get it!"
Stephen Fry, TV personality (and popular twitterer)

"Suddenly, it seems as though all the world's a-twitter"
Newsweek

"Twitter is a way of making sure you are permanently connected to somebody and somebody is permanently connected to you, proving that you are alive. It's like when a parent goes into a child's room to check the child is still breathing. It is a giant baby monitor"
Alain de Botton, author

chapter 1:
getting started
on twitter

New to Twitter? Don't worry – it's really easy to get going. Here's our step by step guide to the Twitterverse.

So what's Twitter all about?

Twitter helps lots of people stay in touch by telling one another what they are doing or thinking. Users (twitterers) post bite-size messages (tweets) for other people to read (follow). They, in turn, can follow the messages posted by anyone else they are interested in staying in touch with. Sometimes called micro-blogging, it's a bit like writing and reading a diary that is always left open to everyone.

What's the point?

You might not think you want or need to read what your friends or family are doing all the time. But it's nice to know! Twitter helps people feel connected with each other, and gives you little glimpses of what others are up to or how they are feeling. It brings you closer to the people you care about.

What do I need to use it?

All you need is a computer with internet access and – if you want to use Twitter when you're on the move – a mobile phone.

How do I get started?

It's simple and takes minutes. Just go to www.twitter.com and click the 'Get Started' button. You'll need to fill in your name and email address, and create a user name or handle for yourself. Add a password to protect your account and you're away. Use your real and full name so that other people can search for you easily.

What do I do now?

Try posting your first tweet! Type straight into the 'What are you doing?' box and click 'update'. Remember that each tweet is limited to 140 characters.

What shall I tweet about?

Anything! People tweet about everything from what they've had for breakfast to their deepest thoughts. Twitter users love to hear what everyone else is doing – even if it seems really boring to you.

Why can I only write 140 characters?

The idea is that people post short messages but post them often. It's like texting in public, so the 140 character limit is roughly the same length you get on your mobile phone texts. You'll soon get an idea of what you can write in 140 characters, and a character counter will tell you how much space you've got left. And remember you can write as often as you like.

How do I find my friends on Twitter?

Once your account is set up, Twitter will let you search for people you know by name. You can also import friends from your email accounts or other networks, or invite them to join Twitter by automatically emailing them. Twitter can also suggest popular users you might like to follow.

How do I start following my friends' posts?

Whenever you find a Twitter user you want to stay in touch with, click their

'Follow' button. You'll then become a follower of them and be able to see their Twitter updates every time you log on. Tweets appear in real time on your home page, so you'll see them as soon as they are posted.

And how do my friends follow my posts?

The same way you follow theirs. They click the 'Follow' button on your profile page and then receive your Twitter updates on their home pages.

How do I know if someone is following me?

Twitter automatically emails you whenever someone decides to follow you. You can change your email preferences if you don't want to receive these emails. On your profile page, if you click 'followers', you will see who is following you.

Can I stop people following me?

Yes – it's easy to put a block on those following your tweets. Go to the Twitter Support section of the Twitter site for help.

Can I follow celebrities?

Yes! One of the best things about Twitter is being able to see what the stars are writing about. But beware of fakes – people pretending to be someone they're not. Use the guide to celebs' addresses (Chapter 7) to find your favourites – all guaranteed genuine!

How do I keep track of who I'm following and being followed by?

On the right of your home and profile pages you'll see the numbers and names of everyone you're in touch with – who is following you and who you are following. Click on any of them to go straight to their profile pages.

How do I see what everyone on Twitter is posting?

Click on the 'Everyone' tab on the home page to see posts from every Twitter user in the world in real time.

There will be more posts than you can ever read, but it can be fun to eavesdrop for a bit.

I'm getting too many tweets to read – help!

Don't feel you have to read everything. Twitter is great to dip in and out of as the mood takes you. If you want to reduce the number of tweets, stop following some users or adjust your settings so you only see messages from certain people.

Can I reply to people's messages?

Yes, by using the @Replies format. By putting the @ symbol before someone's user name, you can send a public

reply that will also be sent to his or her
@Replies box for their attention. Replies
to your own tweets can be found in
your own @Replies box.

How do I send private messages?

Click on the 'Direct Message' tab. You
can only send these private messages
to someone who follows you.

How do I tweet from my mobile?

First you have to set up your phone.
Click on the 'Device updates' tab on
your home page and follow the easy
instructions. Then put Twitter's number
into your phone's address book. Any
text messages that you send to that
number will then immediately appear

on Twitter, just like your computer updates. You can also set up your phone so that it receives other users' updates, too.

What happens if I post a message by mistake?

Tough! Once a tweet is sent it can't be edited.

How do I change my Twitter profile?

Click the 'Settings' tab on your home page, and then the 'Design' tab. You can then upload a photo for your profile, change your page background and more.

Does all this cost anything?

No – Twitter is free. You'll have to pay your normal text message prices for any updates from your mobile phone though.

Where can I get more help?

This book covers the basics of Twitter, but there's lots more to learn. The Twitter site's Support section has answers to lots of common questions. And fellow Twitter users will often be able to help you out if you post a query.

chapter 2:
a short history
of twitter

How did Twitter start? The first version of it was launched in San Francisco in America in 2006. It was the brainwave of a group of people who wanted to discover a simple way of finding out what their friends were doing. Twitter became an instant hit, and the founders – three whizz kid Americans called Biz Stone, Jack Dorsey and Evan Williams – decided to buy it from the company and investors who had previously controlled it. They started adding on new applications and fine-tuning the service, working it up into the site we see today. They took their site's name from the chirping or twittering of birds, which they think is a bit like humans sharing short bits of information with each other.

Just a few years on, Twitter has become an internet craze. By spring 2009 close to ten million people had signed up around the world, and the number is rocketing by the day. The people behind it are still thinking of lots of new ways to use Twitter and add interesting things to its basic service. One of the eventual aims will be to make money from the site, though many users enjoy the fact that it's a free service used for socialising rather than business or advertising.

twitter

v. a succession of light chirping sounds

n. a state of great excitement

chapter 3:
use twitter to...

The great thing about Twitter is that it's as simple or as complicated as you want it to be. People use it for all sorts of different reasons. Here are fifteen of the most popular ones.

● **See what people are doing**
Wondering what your friends or family are up to at the moment? Twitter will show you in an instant.

● **Get something off your chest**
Twitter is a great outlet for your frustrations. Tweet a rant and instantly feel calmer!

- **Stay in touch with groups**

  If you've got a group of friends who regularly gets together, you could tweet ideas for where and when to meet next. You can adjust your settings so that some tweets are only seen by certain people in your groups.

- **Find old friends**

  Look up people you've lost touch with – old school friends, distant relations, former work colleagues and so on.

- **Make new friends**

  Various sites will help you find twitterers with similar interests.

Twittering has even been known to lead to real-life romance!

● **Follow celebs**
Twitter lets you find out what your favourite celebs are up to. Use the guide in this book (Chapter 7) to find some of the most famous twitterers.

● **Get advice**
If you need some tips about something or just the answer to a question that's been bugging you, your followers might be able to enlighten you.

- **Keep track of news**

  Lots of newspapers and magazines offer Twitter feeds to give you snippets of big news as it breaks.

- **Market a business**

  More and more companies are finding that Twitter is a great way of building a brand and staying in touch with customers.

- **Write a poem or story**

  Feeling creative? Write a short story in 140 character instalments, or see if you can fit a little poem into one tweet.

● Make notes

If ideas occur to you while out and about, tweet them from your mobile and be reminded of them later.

● Promote an event

Think of Twitter as a noticeboard for events that all your friends will see. If you're organising a party or a sale, for instance, tweet the details to spread the word.

● Sell something

Ads in newspapers can be expensive, but you can tweet them for free! Post brief details of anything you want to sell, and see who responds.

● Raise some money for charity

If you're taking part in a fundraising event or activity, ask your followers to sponsor you. If you can, include a web link so that they can donate online.

● Pretend to work

Networking and sharing information over Twitter is good for work or study, right?

chapter 4:
top twitter tips

Once you've understood the basics of Twitter, there are plenty of things you can do to turn yourself into an expert twitterer. These ten ideas might get you started.

- **Jazz up your profile**
  Upload a picture of yourself and spend a bit of time making a nice background for your home page. Websites such as www.twitbacks.com and www.mytweetspace.com offer great free help.

- **Learn the Twitter commands**
  Twitter has lots of short-cut commands that you can use to

make your tweeting more fun. Get to know them at the Help section of the Twitter website.

● **Manage your tweets better**
You can change your desktop to keep on top of your tweet feeds and followers. Try sites like www.tweetdeck.com, www.twhirl.com and www.twitterfox.com.

● **Get some more followers**
Spread the word that you're on Twitter and you'll soon see your number of followers rocketing. Tell all your friends and family, and post your Twitter address on things like

your email. Tweeting in peak times – like early evenings – might also attract more people to you.

● **Tweet some photos**

Don't forget that you can share pics as well as words. Websites like www.twitpic.com make it dead easy to upload your photos to Twitter.

● **Find some twitterers near you**

Go to www.nearbytweets.com and see who else might be tweeting from your city, town or village. You might be surprised who you find!

- **Categorise your tweets**

  If you're tweeting about a certain subject, try putting '#' in front of that subject (e.g. #Obama). It will make your post much more visible to anyone else who's interested in that subject.

- **Store up tweets for later**

  If you're going to be away from your computer or phone, you can still tweet by setting up posts to automatically appear at whatever time you like. Go to www.tweetlater.com.

- ## Shrink your links

  Want to tweet a link to another website but haven't got space in your 140 characters? Use an address shrinking service like www.tinyurl.com or www.bit.ly.

- ## Meet up in real life

  Use Twitter to organise a 'tweet-up' of your old friends, or get together a group of new mates you've made on Twitter.

chapter 5:
twitterquette

Not sure what's acceptable and what's not on Twitter? Need some help to become a master tweeter? Here's a guide to ten dos and ten don'ts of Twitter life.

DO post often. People want to hear from you, so don't go quiet!

DON'T feel obliged to fill up the full 140 characters every time you tweet. Keep it short and sweet.

DO think before you post. You can't get a tweet back once it's gone, so think carefully before you hit the button!

DON'T follow too many people. If you've got more than a hundred or so, it's impossible to keep up with their tweets. Concentrate on the people you really want to hear from.

DO spread out your tweets. Posting everything in one go is a bit too much to read, so try to divide things out over a day.

DON'T worry that what you post will be boring. Twitter users love reading even the tiniest bits of your life – like what you've had for lunch!

DO think about your followers and what they might want to read. Try to entertain them. See Chapter 10!

DON'T attack anyone. They'll soon stop following you and your other followers might not be impressed either. Tweet others as you would like to be tweeted!

DO feel free to follow any celebs you're interested in. It's not stalking – honest!

DON'T write like you text. Twitterers generally use full words rather than the sort of short cuts you'd use when texting. So write 'later' instead of 'l8r'.

DO feel free to ask questions when you tweet. Someone might have the answer for you.

DON'T tweet personal details. Unless you want your house to be burgled, avoid revealing your address if you're about to go on holiday, for instance!

DO be yourself. Express your true feelings and not just the things you think people want to hear.

DON'T pretend to be someone else. Especially not celebs – you'll get found out!

DO remember that, unless you Direct Message someone, everyone is watching. There are no private conversations or secrets on Twitter!

DON'T keep following someone if you don't want to. Any user can stop following any other user at any time.

DO be polite and give credit if you're tweeting something someone else has tweeted you. Simply put RT (ReTweet) and the original poster's name at the start of the post.

DON'T self-promote too much. Twitter users get fed up with spam or advertisements, so be careful not to push things on people.

DO block mass followers. Anyone who follows thousands of people but only has a few followers themselves is probably trying to flog you something.

DON'T twitter from the toilet. That's probably taking the Twitter obsession a bit too far. If this applies to you, check out Chapter 11: You know you're addicted to Twitter when...

chapter 6:
top twitterers

The ten most followed twitterers in the world (as of March 2009):

Twitterer	Twitter handle @
1. CNN Breaking News	cnnbrk
2. Britney Spears	britneyspears
3. Barack Obama	barackobama
4. Ashton Kutcher	aplusk
5. Jimmy Fallon	jimmyfallon
6. Shaquille O'Neal	the_real_shaq
7. New York Times	nytimes
8. Lance Armstrong	lancearmstrong
9. Al Gore	algore
10. John Mayer	johncmayer

As is the nature of these things, this list will be forever changing.

chapter 7:
twitter celebs'
address book

Want to know which celebs you can follow on Twitter? Know someone famous is on there but can't find their profile? Here's a handy guide to more than a hundred of the biggest twittering celebs. To find their home pages just type www.twitter.com/ followed by the handle – for instance, www.twitter.com/lilyroseallen.

Celeb	Twitter handle @
Lily Allen	lilyroseallen
Peter Andre	mrpeterandre
Lance Armstrong	lancearmstrong
Richard Bacon	richardpbacon
David Baddiel	ronskanky
Bill Bailey	realbillbailey
Danny Baker	greennowhere

Drew Barrymore	drew_barrymore
Bjork	bjork
Tony Blackburn	tonyblackburn
David Blaine	xblaine
Charley Boorman	charleyboorman
Edith Bowman	edibow
Frankie Boyle	frankieboyle
Russell Brand	rustyrockets
Richard Branson	richardbranson
Derren Brown	browntowers
Gordon Brown	downingstreet
Rob Brydon	realrobbrydon
Mariah Carey	mariahhbf
Will Carling	willcarling
Alan Carr	alancarr
Jimmy Carr	jimmycarr
50 Cent	50cent
John Cleese	johncleese

Coldplay	coldplay
Justin Lee Collins	justinillusion
Fearne Cotton	fearnecotton
Jamie Cullum	jamiecullum
Jean-Claude van Damme	jcvd
Paul Daniels	thepauldaniels
Alan Davies	alandavies1
Michelle Dewberry	michelledewbs
P Diddy	iamdiddy
Snoop Dogg	snoopdogg
Jenni Falconer	jennifalconer
Jimmy Fallon	jimmyfallon
Fall Out Boy	falloutboy
Vanessa Feltz	vanessaonair
Jane Fonda	janefonda
Stephen Fry	stephenfry
Liam Gallagher	liamgallagher
George Galloway	georgegalloway

Peaches Geldof	peaches_g
Dave Gorman	dave_gorman
Calvin Harris	calvinharris
Tony Hawk	tonyhawk
Chesney Hawkes	chesneyhawkes
Richard Herring	herring1967
Perez Hilton	perezhilton
Matthew Horne	mfhorne
Eddie Izzard	eddieizzard
Boris Johnson	mayoroflondon
Dom Joly	domjoly
Jordan	misskatieprice
Judge Jules	realjudgejules
Phill Jupitus	jupitusphillip
Ronan Keating	ronanofficial
Hardeep Singh Kohli	hardeepdeepdeep
Ashton Kutcher	aplusk

Kate Lawler	katelawler
Iain Lee	iainlee
Robert Llewellyn	bobbyllew
Courtney Love	courtneylover79
Matt Lucas	realmattlucas
Ludacris	ludajuice
John Mayer	johncmayer
Katie Melua	katiemelua
Kylie Minogue	kylie_minogue
David Mitchell	realdmitchell
Demi Moore	mrskutcher
Chris Moyles	chrisdjmoyles
Andy Murray	andy_murray
Graham Norton	grahamnorton
Barack Obama	barackobama
Jamie Oliver	jamie_oliver
Shaquille O'Neal	the_real_shaq
Yoko Ono	yokoono

Katy Perry	katyperry
Andi Peters	xxandip
Pet Shop Boys	petshopboys
Michael Phelps	michael_phelps
Billie Piper	billiepiper
Dawn Porter	hotpatootie
John Prescott	johnprescott
Daniel Radcliffe	danielradcliffe
Dizzee Rascal	dizzeerascal
Joan Rivers	joanriversqvc
Jon Ronson	jonronson
Jonathan Ross	wossy
Borat Sagdiyev	borat
Phillip Schofield	schofe
Arnold Schwarzenegger	schwarzenegger
Mike Skinner	skinnermike
Britney Spears	britneyspears

Martha Stewart	marthastewart
Donnie Wahlberg	donniewahlberg
Danny Wallace	misterwallace
Robert Webb	realrobertwebb
Holly Willoughby	hollywills
Claudia Winkleman	claudiawinkle
Reggie Yates	regyates

chapter 8: wossy's best tweets

Jonathan Ross is one of the most active and funny celeb twitterers. Here are some of his best tweets, all posted within a few months in 2009.

"Morning has broken rather beautifully in London. Sun streaming through the windows, birds singing outside, then I step barefoot in dog poo."

"One of the dogs threw up last night and is making weird faces. Will take him to the vet. Might get myself checked out while I'm there."

"Am trying to find enough energy to go out. Maybe stay in and watch wife twitter instead :)"

"Just got back from collecting the kids from school. Walked all 6 dogs up there on my own. Now need long rest."

"My wife just walked in without knocking and caught me dancing to Lionel Richie and the Commodores – Machine Gun. Slight shame. Goodnight."

"Just came back from the gym and a swim. Decided to be virtuous. Then ate chicken and bacon followed by hazlenut chocolate. WTF!!!!"

"I am going to bed. Jane is reading a new horror novel. I will now spoil it by chatting inanely at her while she tries to finish chapter."

"Best ice cream flavour I ever tasted – black sesame seed!!!!"

"Just read Mens Health magazine on the loo before going to work. Does that count as going to the gym?"

"I have eaten too much fish pie with Jane. Must lie down while body digests. Look boa constrictor having swallowed a football. Not pretty."

"My wife and I just finished off the chocolate fountain that she set up for

Honeys birthday. Am now sweating like Stephen Fry on a treadmill."

"I just got beaten twice at pool. By a 14 year old and a 17 year old. Neither of them are especially good. Time for a nap I think."

"My wife and her friend are having St Tropez tan applied upstairs. I am going to spy on them, like Bill Oddie on Springwatch."

"Brain is sending command to body. Get up and go to gym."

chapter 9: twit-tastic true stories

Twitter makes the news

In January 2009, when a US Airways plane crash landed on the Hudson River in New York, the first news of it was broken via Twitter. One on-the-spot user immediately tweeted: "There's a plane in the Hudson. I'm on the ferry going to pick up the people. Crazy." Other users posted updates as everyone on the plane was rescued, and the first pictures of the scene were posted via TwitPic. The amazing incident made many people aware of Twitter for the first time.

A tweet too far

American star Jennifer Aniston was reported to have split up with her boyfriend in early 2009 because he spent too much time twittering. Singer John Mayer allegedly said he was too busy to talk to Aniston on the phone – but still found time to tweet regularly. "Jen was fuming," one newspaper reported a friend as saying. "There he was, telling her he didn't have time for her, and yet his page was filled with updates!"

Lift me out of here

TV star Stephen Fry, one of the most popular celebs on Twitter (and it's easy to see why), once posted an update while stuck in a lift. "Hell's teeth," he tweeted from his mobile. "We could be here for hours. Arse, poo and widdle."

Fry then posted updates and photos until he and his fellow lift passengers were rescued.

Demi's bum deal

Twitter often reveals celebs doing everyday chores like the rest of us. But American actress Demi Moore wasn't expecting what she found posted by her husband Ashton Kutcher – a photo of her doing the laundry in her underwear. The picture has become one of Twitter's most viewed postings. Apparently, Moore and Kutcher have both admitted to being addicted to Twitter, and once got into trouble for posting complaints about their neighbour's building work.

Online breakup

Celebs have used Twitter to reveal big personal news. In early 2009 Madonna revealed, during a chat with fans on the site, that she had split up with her boyfriend. "Hello Madonna honey, am glad you are single again – you made your best music as a single woman," tweeted one fan to Madonna. "Not as glad as I am!" she replied.

Home tweet home

Some people worry that Twitter has taken over their lives. But few would take their obsession as far as one San Francisco user did when his house was broken into. Instead of phoning the police, he tweeted his followers.

twitter: a pocket guide

"I swear a random dude just walked into my bathroom and I can't believe I haven't freaked out," he wrote. As the drunken burglar passed out, the twitterer continued to post updates.

The royal twitterer

Twitter users are in grand company – even the Queen is now the subject of tweets. London's famous Westminster Abbey has its own Twitter profile – wabbey – and has had regular posts and photos from visits there by Her Majesty. "The Queen is wearing a lovely turquoise hat and cream coat" ran one of them.

Top twits

Controversial comedian Russell Brand is arguably the most self-obsessed twitterer in celeb-land. Based on an analysis of the number of followers a celeb has compared to the number of people he or she follows, Brand leads the list ahead of singers Katy Perry and Lily Allen, actor Ashton Kutcher and DJ Chris Moyles.

The youngest follower

Twitter has users of all ages – but the youngest ever twitterer started the habit before he was even born. Tyler Menscher's mum in New York designed a special belt containing sensors to record when he was kicking from the womb – or chat-womb, as it might be called. These triggered automatic updates to his parent's Twitter feeds.

Love libel

Lots of users like to get things off their chest on Twitter, but be careful who you offend! The first ever Twitter libel action was brought against American rock star Courtney Love after she posted several tweets criticising her former fashion designer. The court claim in Los Angeles said Love had carried out "an obsessive and delusional crusade" on Twitter and other sites.

Courtroom twit

The verdict in a court trial in America was appealed after it emerged that someone on the jury had twittered about the case. A company that had been ordered to pay out $12m after the trial later appealed when it found that one of the jurors had tweeted eight times from his mobile phone. He had suggested that his friends didn't buy shares in the firm as "they'll probably cease to exist, now that their wallet is $12m lighter."

Twittered out of jail

James Buck, a student from California, used Twitter to help get out of jail in

Egypt. After being taken into custody while reporting on a protest against the country's government, he managed to tweet one word – "arrested" – to his followers from his mobile phone. Within hours, his friends had organised a petition and contacted influential people to help get him released.

Lessons in Twitter

School children in England could one day learn about Twitter in their classrooms. In 2009, a draft review of what children learn in school suggested that knowing how to use social networking sites like Twitter could help children when they get older. That would mean five to 11 year olds learning how to write in sentences of 140 characters or less...

Twitfest

Twitter users around the world got together for the first ever 'Twestival' early in 2009. More than 200 cities around the world organised get-togethers of twitterers, allowing many of them to meet each other in real life for the first time. Edinburgh and Glasgow in Scotland both drew hundreds of people. Worldwide, the Twestival raised about quarter of a million pounds for charity.

The Twitter ghosts

If you think you're too busy to tweet sometimes, you might follow the example of celebs like Britney Spears and find someone to do it for you! Apparently, Spears is one of several well known twitterers who have assistants or ghost writers to tweet on their behalf.

"It's 140 characters. If you need a ghostwriter for that, I feel sorry for you." *American basketball player Shaquille O'Neal on celebs using Twitter ghostwriters*

Cooking up a tweet

Cooking from Twitter might seem a bit difficult when you've only got 140 characters for a recipe. But celebrity chefs are rising to the challenge, tweeting simple instructions for some tasty dishes. Here's one, from Michelin-starred Angela Hartnett for a tomato sauce for pasta: "Heat 4T olvoil + onion/ squashplumtoms/ tompuree/ garl/ sug/ rosemary. Remv rosemary. Heat low30m. +Oil to srv." Need a translation? "Heat four tablespoons of olive oil. Add chopped onion, then squashed plum tomatoes, tomato puree, garlic, sugar and rosemary. Remove the rosemary after a while then simmer on a low heat for 30 minutes. Add olive oil to serve."

chapter 10:
twit wit

Twittering jokes is a great way to keep your friends laughing and find new followers. Here are some great jokes for you to tweet yourself – all under the magic 140 character limit!

☺

A sandwich walks into a bar. The barman says: "Sorry, we don't serve food here!"

☺

What's brown and sticky? A stick

☺

What do you call a woman with one leg? Eileen

What do you call a man with no arms and no legs in a pool? Bob

☺

What do you call a man with no arms and no legs sitting by your front door? Matt

☺

Did you hear about the man who lost his left arm and left leg in an accident? He's all right now

What lies at the bottom of the sea and bites its nails? A nervous wreck

☺

Why don't cannibals eat clowns? Because they taste funny

☺

What do you call a dog with no legs? Nothing – he's not going to come no matter what you call

☺

What do you say to a one legged hitch-hiker? Hop in

☺

A policeman spots a woman driving whilst knitting. He drives alongside her and shouts "Pull over!" "No," she shouts, "It's a scarf!"

☺

What do you call an elephant with a machine gun? Sir

☺

Two cows in a field. "What do you think of this mad cow disease?" asks one. "Don't ask me, I'm a sheep!"

☺

What do you give a man who has everything? Penicillin

☺

Did you hear about the man who injured himself tap dancing? He fell off and twisted his ankle on the sink

☺

Two fish in a tank. One says to the other:
"Do you know how to drive this?"

☺

"Doctor, I think I've got amnesia. What
should I do?" "Try to forget about it."

☺

"Doctor, I feel like a pair of curtains."
"Pull yourself together!"

☺

Why do giraffes have long necks?
Because they have smelly feet

☺

What's a pirate's favourite letter? R

☺

What did the big chimney say to the little chimney? "You're too young to smoke!"

☺

Where do elephants go to lie down? Anywhere they like

☺

What do you call a group of cows with a sense of humour? A laughing stock

☺

Two men walk into a bar. You'd have thought one of them would have seen it

☺

Do you want to hear a dirty joke? OK. A white horse fell in the mud

☺

If at first you don't succeed, redefine
success

☺

I married Miss Right. I just didn't know
her first name was Always

☺

Hard work never hurt anyone. But why
take a chance?

☺

Always give 100% in a week at work.
25% on Monday and Tuesday, 20% on
Wednesday and Thursday, and 10% on
Friday

☺

If something is worth doing, it would have been done already

☺

When blondes have more fun, do they know it?

☺

Hard work pays off in the future. Being lazy pays off now

☺

For sale: parachute. Only used once, never opened, small stain

☺

Did you hear that they've taken the word gullible out of the dictionary?

☺

If money doesn't grow on trees, why do banks have branches?

☺

The sooner you fall behind, the longer you have to catch up

☺

Change is inevitable. Except when you're using a vending machine

☺

Always remember that you are unique – just like everyone else

☺

The difference between genius and stupidity is that genius has its limits

chapter 11:
you know you're
addicted to
twitter when...

Let's face it – Twitter can be pretty addictive. If you recognise more than half of these 20 signs of Twitter cravings, the chances are you're officially hooked!

- The first thing you do after you wake up is tweet

- You don't talk to your friends unless it's via Twitter

- You tweet everyone what you've just had for lunch

- You get ridiculously excited every time you get a new follower

- You check your Twitter feed before you go to bed. Or in bed

- You put your Twitter handle on your business card

- You find yourself getting angry when the Twitter site goes down

- You have to log out of Twitter before you get any work done on your computer

- You type @ in front of people's names, even when you're not on Twitter

- You tweet on the toilet

- You tweet from a hospital

- Your mother joined Twitter just so she could talk to you again

- You hear tweets in your sleep

- The @ button on your keypad is getting worn out

- You stop using sites like Facebook and MySpace

- You start to think celeb users like Stephen Fry and Britney Spears are your best friends

- You ask someone to repeat a joke so you can tweet it

- You start speaking only in sentences of 140 characters or less

- You go to the doctor's because your thumbs are so sore

- You've bought this book

chapter 12:
twit talk:
a twictionary

Baffled by some of the terms on Twitter? Need to know what DM stands for or want to find the word for drunken twittering? Here's a very handy Twictionary to get you speaking fluent Twittish in no time.

140er

A tweet that uses exactly the maximum 140 characters

atwaction

A crush on another twitterer

bgd

Short for the background on your profile page

block

To stop someone's tweets appearing in your feed

celebritweet

A post from a celebrity on Twitter

chirp

A tweet

chirpes

Condition caused by too much tweeting

detweet

A tweet written but then deleted

DM
Direct Message

drive-by-tweet
A quick tweet posted in between other jobs

dweet
Tweet sent while drunk

egotweetical
Someone who tweets about themselves far too much

exectweets
Businesses and business people on Twitter

fail whale

The friendly whale that appears on Twitter when the site is down

faker

User posing as someone (usually a celebrity) they're not

follower

User who follows another's tweets

handle

Your Twitter name, beginning with @

illtwiterate

Describes someone who doesn't understand Twitter

IM

Instant Message

micro-blogging

Another phrase for tweeting

mistweet

An error in a tweet, or a tweet you later regret

nudge

A friendly reminder to someone to update a profile

qwitter

Twitter quitter – someone who stops using it

retweet
Posting something already posted by another user

speedtweet
A quick post

speets
Spam tweets

twadd
To add someone as a follower

twaddle
Boring tweets

twaffic
Twitter traffic

twaggle
Gaggle or group of followers

twaiting
Twittering while waiting, or waiting for someone to twitter

twammer
Twitter spammer

twead
To read a twitter

tweaming
Dreaming about Twitter. Usually a sign you're addicted

tweavesdropping
Reading strangers' Twitter conversations

tweek
Twitter geek

tweekend
A weekend spent twittering

tweepish
To feel sheepish about something you tweeted

tweet
A post on Twitter

tweetaholic
Someone who is addicted to Twitter

tweet cred
A popular or trendy twitterer will have this

tweeter
A Twitter user

tweeteritis
Illness caused by too much twittering – sore fingers, for example

tweetheart
Someone you fall in love with while tweeting

tweet out
To sign out

tweetspeak
The language of Twitter

tweet up
Meeting up with users in real life

twego
Twitter ego

twehab
Rehab from Twitter – an enforced break

twendy
Something trendy on Twitter

tweople
Twitter users

twerd

Twitter nerd

twhiner

User who only tweets when there's something to moan about

twhore

Someone who will do anything to get attention on Twitter

twibute

A compliment paid to a fellow user

twiffle

Boring or daft post – Twitter twaffle

twinterview
Interview conducted on Twitter

twired
Exhausted from too much twittering

twirlfriend
A Twitter girlfriend

twirting
Flirting over Twitter

twitch
The need to tweet

twitlit
Stories or poems posted via Twitter

twitology
The study of all things Twitter

twit-tastic
Great twittering

twitteraphobe
Someone who doesn't like Twitter or is afraid of it

twitterati
The A-list celeb twitterers

twitterature
The collected twitterings of a user

twittercide
Killing off your Twitter account

twitterite
A Twitter user

twitterquette
Proper etiquette and good manners on Twitter

twitter rage
Rage over a post

twittersphere
The community of twitterers

Twitterverse
The wonderful world of Twitter

twittervision
Animated tweet collection, or what you get from too much use

twitticism
Witty tweet

twittilation
Twitter titillation

twittizen
A citizen of Twitter

twittworking
Pretending to work by 'networking' on Twitter

twoetry
Poem posted by Twitter

twoosh
A post of exactly 140 characters

twuck it
Twitter swearing

twyping
Typing a tweet

unfollow
To stop following a user

winggers
Twitter fingers

chapter 13:
useful websites

Need more help with Twitter? Want to pimp your profile and applications? These sites are here to help you.

Twitter
The original site!
www.twitter.com

Valebrity
Check whether that celeb you've found on Twitter is real or fake
www.valebrity.com

Just Tweet It
Great site for finding twitterers similar to you
www.justtweetit.com

Nearby Tweets

Find out who's twittering close to you

www.nearbytweets.com

Twestival

Worldwide real-life gathering of Twitter
users to raise money for charity

www.twestival.com

TwitPic

Allows you to post and view photos via
Twitter

www.twitpic.com

Twittervision

See where in the world people are
twittering from

www.twittervision.com

Tweetstats

Measure your Twitter use and make graphs

www.tweetstats.com

Tweetlater

All sorts of fun Twitter extras, including a facility to let you leave tweets to be posted later on

www.tweetlater.com

Tweet What You Eat

Helps you keep a diary of what you eat each day via Twitter. Great if you're trying to stick to a diet!

www.tweetwhatyoueat.com

Twitter Job Search

Find work just a tweet away!

www.twitterjobsearch.com

Bigger Twitter

Lets you post messages longer than the usual 140 characters

www.biggertwitter.com

Tweetwasters

Work out how much time you're wasting on Twitter!

www.tweetwasters.com

Twitbacks

Free backgrounds to jazz up your profile

www.twitbacks.com

SnapTweet

Site for sharing Flickr photos on Twitter
www.snaptweet.com

We Follow

Great directory of Twitter users, tagged
by areas like music, celebrity, politics
and sport.
www.wefollow.com

Twellow

Like a Yellow Pages for Twitter users
and services
www.twellow.com

Twitter Addict

Add your name to the list of Twaddicts!
www.twitaddict.com

Twitterholic

Up to date lists of the 100 twitterers with the most followers
www.twitterholic.com

Twit This

Site to help visitors to a website or blog post a link to it direct to Twitter
www.twitthis.com

Friend or Follow

Find out which users you are following
who aren't following you back
www.friendorfollow.com

Mr Tweet

Personal assistant to help you find new
people to follow
www.mrtweet.net

Tweetbeep

A site that will alert you whenever you
have been twittered about
www.tweetbeep.com

"We'd like to thank you in 140 characters or less. And we just did!"

Twitter co-founder Jack Dorsey on picking up an award for his company

Crombie Jardine books are available from Amazon and most good bookshops.

www.crombiejardine.com

www.twitter.com/crombiejardine

CHAT ROOM WIND-UPS
ISBN 978-1-906051-17-4, £4.99, PB, 2009

weird websites

Stuart McLean

WEIRD WEBSITES
ISBN 978-1-906051-29-7, £4.99, PB, 2009

the little eBay book

UNOFFICIAL   UNOFFICIAL

The website's most weird and wondrous...

THE LITTLE EBAY BOOK
ISBN 1-905102-19-4, £2.99, PB